A souvenir guide

Buckland Abbey
Devon

Annie Bullen

G000240741

A Place of Prayer	2
Amicia's gift	4
A new monastery	6
Building Buckland	8
Daily life	10
Working the land	12
Treasures in store	14
Establishing an order	16
Rise and fall	18
Home of the Rich and Famous	20
An ambitious man	22
Sir Richard's domestic designs	24
Sir Richard sets sail once more	26
Bought by the nation's darling	28
The Drakes at Buckland	30
Buckland's swashbuckling hero	32
Changes Over Time	34
Estate details	36
Georgian restoration	38
Marshall's measures	40
Farmyard design	42
Keeping the character	44
Times of great change	46
Rescued for the nation	48
Completing the picture	50
As Tranquil Today	52
The abbey's gardens	54
A lasting peace	56

National Trust

A Place of Prayer

Our story starts towards the end of the 13th century, with a rich and titled widow devoting her life to building a monastery deep in the Devon countryside.

Buckland Abbey, founded in 1278 for the 'white monks' of the Cistercian order, prospered for more than two and a half centuries. Its rich lands were farmed by the monks, who stored the fruits of their labours in the enormous barn that still stands today (its cathedral-like interior adorning our front cover). The monks immersed themselves in a life of work, prayer and silent contemplation in this peaceful place, helping the poor and infirm, and following the austere lifestyle dictated by their founding fathers.

Dissolution and conversion

Everything changed with the Dissolution. The monks were forced to leave their monastery in 1538 when the last abbot, John Toker, surrendered it to King Henry VIII.

Three years later the abbey, along with its many secular buildings and land, became the property of the Grenville family of Bideford. Eventually, Sir Richard Grenville – soldier, ship's captain and a man of energy and passion – converted the abbey church into a mansion.

Sir Richard later sold his house to another great seafarer, and the nation's darling, Sir Francis Drake, enormously wealthy from Spanish plunder and royal reward.

The abbey's fortunes fluctuated from gentle decline to renovation in the centuries following Drake's death in 1596. But those early monks and their founder, Amicia, would still recognise this quiet place, set in its peaceful valley, which has changed relatively little since they arrived here more than seven hundred years ago.

Left The luxuriant landscape around Buckland Abbey

Amicia's gift

The gift of land that supported the foundation of an abbey at Buckland was considerable, amounting to more than 8,000 hectares (20,000 acres). This act of generosity by an extremely wealthy but heirless widow ensured the continuation of her name.

Amicia de Redvers, dowager Countess of Devon, the daughter and widow of wealthy and powerful men, had lost her brother and her only son in 1262, poisoned at the same dinner table by power-hungry barons.

Amicia's daughter, Isabella de Fortibus, Countess of Albemarle and Devon, also widowed, was in possession of large tracts of land around Buckland. Having no children to inherit her fortune, she signed the land over to her elderly mother for the foundation of a Cistercian abbey.

Amicia's motivation for granting this gift of land was so that the monks might intercede for the health of the souls of her family, past, present and future. Amicia requested that brothers should be sent from Quarr, an Isle of Wight abbey dear to her heart, founded almost 150 years earlier by her late husband's ancestors.

Right This carving was at one time believed to represent Amicia de Redvers; while her identity is not known, she is original to the monastery founded by Amicia

Support for the Cistercians

It is a fair assumption that Amicia visited Buckland Abbey and perhaps even stayed here, in the guesthouse once it was built. It is also likely that it was she who provided the necessary 'starter buildings', where the brothers could sleep and worship until the masons and other builders had finished the church and the dormitories.

Once the abbey was established, regular visits were made by abbots of Buckland's 'motherhouse' at Quarr. The visiting abbot stayed for three days, assessing the spiritual and material health of the abbey, giving fatherly advice and, if necessary, criticism. These visits are recorded in an early 14th-century manuscript, the 'Buckland Book', now in the British Library.

Below Cistercian monks at an abbey in France

Below left St Benedict delivering his rule to the monks of his order

The seeds of Cistercianism

The Cistercian order grew from the Benedictine foundation as a reaction against the increasing opulence of many monasteries. In 1098 Robert, Abbot of Molesme, with 20 monks, founded a monastery in the solitude of Cîteaux, in France. They wanted to revive the original spirit of the Rule of St Benedict, observing vows of poverty, chastity and obedience more literally, placing an emphasis on silence, austerity and isolation. By the year 1200 more than 500 Cistercian houses were founded across Europe in remote, often uncultivated, locations.

A new monastery

In 1278 Abbot Robert set out from Quarr with seven monks, rather than the traditional twelve representing Christ and his apostles. He and his small band of monks were bound for Buckland, in a deep Devon valley, where they would build their new monastery.

This lonely valley, reached after several days travelling from their motherhouse at Quarr on the Isle of Wight, offered the tranquillity they sought for their life of prayer and contemplation.

Bounded on its eastern flank by the wild reaches of Dartmoor, it was green with many trees and fertile with water from the encircling rivers Tavy and Walkham. There was pasture for their sheep and, on the slopes, sheltered fields where orchards, filled with neat rows of fruit trees, would soon be flourishing.

Robert's election as abbot and the order to lead this band of founding brothers to build the new monastery at Buckland had happened just weeks earlier. When they set out on this task they could not have known that the Abbey of St Mary and St Benedict at Buckland was to be the last Cistercian house built in Devon.

Right The seal of Buckland Abbey would have been used to authorise and authenticate orders issued by the abbot

Far right Some monks worked while others prayed

Farmer monks

The Cistercians were adept at managing livestock and arable pasture, orchards and fishponds. They were skilled in controlling water in order to power mills. Amicia must have known that her endowment would enable the Cistercians to exploit their skills as farmers and managers of the land to the full. The manors of Buckland, Bickleigh, Walkhampton and Cullompton, together with manorial rights, including rents from tenants and the 'advowsons' (the right to appoint clergy to the parish churches), were given to the monks. Overseeing the inhabitants, the mills, fisheries, woods and moorland, was also their duty. In addition, they were given the Hundred (a medieval term for a certain area) of Roborough, which stretched to the Plymouth Sound. This meant that the Abbot of Buckland became, in effect, Lord of the Hundred, responsible for the administration of criminal and civil justice.

Monastic manpower

Abbot Robert's responsibilities were numerous. In the monastery he would 'occupy the place of Christ' in accordance with their guiding precept, the Rule of St Benedict, but he also had duties in the wider community, including the administration of justice. Assistance came from his deputy, the prior, who would preside in the refectory and organise the daily labour. Robert and his prior sat opposite each other in the choir. The choir monks had chosen to devote their lives to God; they were thinkers, philosophers, scholars and poets, all able to speak and write in Latin and English. Each of Robert's monks had his own place in the choir, dependent on his role and experience. The sub-prior was in charge of discipline and the proper form of worship in the church. Most important to the running of the estate was the cellarer, in effect the business manager, who oversaw the farms or 'granges' and supervised the lay brothers. These men, the conversi, did the heavy lifting and were generally ill educated. From their ranks were drawn those with practical skills – the cooks, smiths, tailors, launderers, farmers and fishermen – necessary for the smooth running of the monastery.

Building Buckland

There was no particular Cistercian architectural style, but the brotherhood's insistence on simplicity informed the design of their first monasteries. By the time Buckland was built, the early austerity and purity of this style had faded. That said, Buckland's late 13th-century abbey followed the plain tradition of the earliest monasteries.

In all their enterprises, the bulk of the physical labour was undertaken by the conversi, who, while not accorded the status of monks, lived with them and took vows of obedience. We do not know whether the conversi built this new Cistercian complex, or travelling masons were engaged to construct the church and its surrounding buildings.

However, there is no doubt where the building materials came from. Stone and timber were local and abundant. Quarries still exist, tucked into the sides of the valley above the church, and from these the slate-like 'shillet', with its distinctive green and brown flecks, was cut to make the stone building blocks. The soaring arches, pillars, doorways and window frames were hewn from the soft granite of nearby Roborough Down, while the timber came from the surrounding woods.

Right Masonry for the abbey originated from the granite quarries of Roborough Down

A complex arrangement

The abbey church, the centre of monastic life, was built in the shape of a cross: the tower low, the nave long, its beauty uncluttered by stained glass, paintings or elaborate carving, which could have distracted the monks from their unceasing dialogue with God.

The cloister, the pivotal point of the abbey, was the gateway to the church and the other chambers of the complex. Usually tucked into the angle of the nave and south transept of the church, it allowed entrance to the book room, sacristy, chapter house, parlour and monks' day room on its eastern side. South of the cloister would be the kitchen and the monks' refectory, while the dining room and day room used by the conversi filled the western range. However, at Buckland this usual pattern was reversed, as the lie of the hilly land dictated that the cloister must be fitted between the nave and the north transept, so all these chambers were constructed on the northern side.

The 'dorters' or dormitories of the choir monks and the conversi ran above their respective buildings. Two sets of stairs led into the choir monks' dormitory. The 'day stairs' rose from the cloister, while 'night stairs' took the brothers directly into the church where, soon after midnight, they stood in the choir for Vigils, the first act of worship of the day.

Between the monks' day room and the parlour and chapter house was the calefactory or warming house where, during the winter, a fire was lit. The monks warmed themselves here in rest periods, such as after Vigils on Christmas night and the warmth would have risen to the dormitory above. It was here that the shoes of the monks were greased, the heat allowing the fats to melt into the leather. Here too the monks were bled – a regular feature of monastic life – after which the weakened monks were allowed extra rations and three days' rest (see over).

The chapter house where the whole community met daily to hear a section of the Rule of St Benedict was, after the church, the most important chamber. Punishment took place here, but it was also where a light was kindled each night so that monks could read and study after they had sung Vigils. They were warned that they must not cover their faces with hoods to hide a surreptitious snooze – sleeping was strictly forbidden. Abbots were accorded the privilege of burial in the chapter house.

Separated from the main abbey complex by a wall, but once part of the monastery, are the Cider House and Tower Cottage. The former possibly housed the infirmary, while Tower Cottage might have been the abbot's house.

Below An example of a Cistercian abbey complex; this one is in Germany

Daily life

Simplicity and austerity were the keynotes of the Cistercian way of life. This applied not only to the monks' daily routine but also to the clothes they wore and the food they ate.

Although Abbot Robert and his brothers were known as 'white monks', their habits, spun from un-dyed wool, could vary in colour from white to grey. Furs, vests and shirts were not allowed but they wore a 'scapula', a wide woollen over-garment rather like a protective apron, when working. A cowl, or hood, covered their heads. Each monk was allowed three tunics, two cowls, two pairs of hose and a scapula.

Once every two weeks the kitchener would heat water, sharpen his scissors and razors and 'tonsure' the monks, shaving a circular patch on their heads and removing beards.

Monks' mealtimes

When not giving haircuts, the kitchener was responsible for cooking the food. The kitchen was situated between the refectories of the monks and the lay brothers. Two conversi worked there on a rota. Their busiest time was Saturday evening, when they scrubbed out the kitchen, the reredorters (the lavatories) and washing troughs, drew water for the Saturday evening foot-washing ritual and collected fuel for the kitchen fire.

Before eating, the brothers washed their hands in troughs, conveniently located outside the refectories. Only novices, young monks and those working in the fields took breakfast, which consisted of a quarter of a loaf of bread and some beer.

Dinner, the main meal of the day, was at noon in summer, followed by supper in the afternoon. In the winter it was served mid-afternoon and was the only meal of the day. It was eaten in silence while the prior read from the Bible. Early Cistercians ate no meat or fat, but these might have been allowed by the time Buckland was built. The very sick or those recovering from a bloodletting session might receive meat (see box). Milk, cheese and eggs were served, as were vegetables, such as peas and beans, and bread, salt and herbs. Fish formed part of the diet and beer or water was drunk. The monks fasted throughout Lent and Advent, eating the bare minimum, to purify their soul and achieve empathy with God.

Above A monk being given a tonsure

Opposite top The monks' day followed a strict schedule; shown is a month's calendar in the first half of the 13th century

Monastic medicine

Bloodletting was generally practised perhaps as a means of purification or redressing an imbalance in the body. However, in monasteries the custom seems to have had a different motivation: bloodletting was a routine practice done for healthy monks – it was not permitted if a monk was ill or at times when the monks would be fasting, such as Advent. The monasteries also prohibited bloodletting during the harvest season when work requirements were much higher. Monasteries had 'customaries', working guides for monks, offering them examples of how to deal with a wide variety of situations. From these texts a few suggestions have been extracted: one reason may be to do with decreasing the 'heat of desire', referring to carnal appetites, be that food or sex; another may have been its spiritual connotations, in imitation of Christ, who was bled during his crucifixion. Lastly, because the parts relating to bloodletting are often found between chapters on general health and personal hygiene, it may be that the practice was considered part of preventative healthcare.

Working the land

Much of the land at Buckland was already in the hands of tenant farmers when the first monks arrived. The Cistercians, known for their skill in farming, developed its productivity still further, planting orchards and a garden.

Cistercians were sheep-farmers of note, known for producing quality wool, and the Buckland flocks were no exception. In 1347 the wool yield was so high that Edward III demanded a levy from Buckland to augment his coffers, depleted by the Hundred Years War against France. Ten years earlier Buckland, deemed vulnerable to attack because of its river access to the sea, had been fortified with crenellations, still seen on part of the chancel roof.

A working estate
Fields were probably dug by the conversi, hedges planted and walls built from the plentiful stone. Further afield, 'granges' or farms were set up, generally for pasturing sheep but also for growing oats, the staple crop, and rye. Cattle grazed on the meadowland while, nearer home, poultry and bees were tended, vegetables and herbs grown, and milk, cheese and butter produced.

The two-storey building that now houses the restaurant and shop was once a stable, although it was converted into a guesthouse by a later owner.

To the north of Tower Cottage and the Cider House lay the 'outer court', the ancillary buildings and workshops such as the bake-house, where considerable numbers of loaves were produced daily, the brew-house and workshops for the masons, tailors, carpenters, smiths, wheelwrights and the dairy. Here, too, were the fishponds, quarries and orchards. As elsewhere in the cloister and in the fields, monks and conversi worked in silence, speaking only when absolutely necessary and often using sign language to make themselves understood.

Above Medieval Cistercian monks ploughing

Opposite A hive in the garden behind the great, buttressed walls of the tithe barn

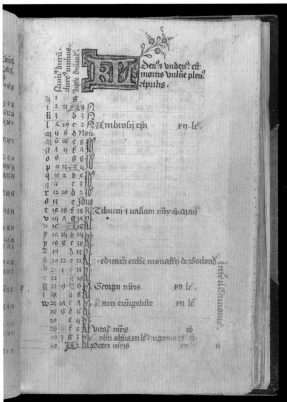

Work, eat, pray, repeat

The rule followed by the brothers emphasised the importance of manual labour, so that the day was divided into worship and work. This followed the seven or eight offices of the Cistercian liturgy, starting with Vigils in the very early hours of the morning, to Lauds at daybreak and thence to Prime, Terce, Sext (noon), None, Vespers and Compline. The Buckland Book shows that the plain Gregorian chant used by the monks, whether in their choir stalls or working in the fields, was in the old style, without any modern additions.

Above A page from the Buckland Book showing the strict routine of the abbey

Treasures in store

It is telling that the most magnificent building at Buckland is the Great Barn, constructed at the same time as the church which it dwarves. The barn was clearly built to serve a richly productive farming community.

The Great Barn provided storage for wool, fleeces, cattle hides, crops such as oats, wheat and other cereals, cheese, flax, honey, beeswax, hay, wood for fencing and firewood, as well as fruit from the orchards. A space would have been left clear by the doors for winnowing, an ancient agricultural method used to separate grain from chaff. In its simplest form it involves throwing the cereal crop into the air so that the wind blows away the chaff, while the grains fall back down.

Abbot Robert's cellarer and maybe some trusted conversi would have had access to the barn. Although the use of these lay brothers was dwindling by the time Buckland was built, there is no doubt they were an important part of the labour force.

Light from narrow ventilation slits between closely set exterior buttresses filters into the shaded and cool interior; medieval pigeon lofts exist above the doors, while the original 'putlog' holes that supported interior scaffolding below the great roof can be seen. It might have been thatched when first built. The arch-braced and pegged oak timbers of the roof were fitted in the 15th century.

Right The magnificent interior of the Great Barn

Buckland Abbey seen from the north; the Great Barn stands out prominently to the left

Establishing an order

Life at the abbey seems to have been, for the most part, peaceful and productive. However, the way was not always smooth for Abbot Robert.

The Bishop of Exeter, Walter Bronescombe, whose diocese covered the whole of Devon and Cornwall, was offended when he heard that Robert, newly arrived at Buckland, had celebrated Mass without his permission. The bishop promptly excommunicated the monks. Only an intercession from Queen Eleanor, presumably contacted by Amicia who remained close to the court of Edward I, persuaded the bishop to relent.

Neighbourly disputes

Another tussle, this time physical, had to be resolved through the legal system. Robert and his monks were taking wood from the banks of the River Tavy to mend a weir when they were confronted by Thomas Gyreband, the forester of the Abbot of Tavistock Abbey, the owners of the wood. A struggle ensued and although Gyreband told the courts that the abbot and his men attacked him with axes, shot an arrow into his arm and stole his coat, the justices preferred Robert's version, that Gyreband had been the assailant as they lawfully cut wood for their repair and that their arrow shot had been in defence. The 'stolen' coat had been dropped and retrieved by the monks as Gyreband fled. The hapless forester was jailed for perjury.

Rise and fall

The success of the Cistercian enterprise, the productivity of the monks and their farming and land-management abilities created great prosperity in the area. However, their wealth and influence brought them and all monasteries to the attention of a king who would be their undoing.

Buckland's abbots were members of the Totnes Merchants' Guild and there is no doubt that outlying farms or 'granges' were established, one as far away as Cullompton in east Devon. At first farmed by conversi under the supervision of a monk, these granges would in later days have been leased to tenants.

In 1317, by which time Abbot Robert had been buried with due reverence inside the chapter house for about 30 years, the tiny village of Buckland was granted not only a weekly market, but also an annual three-day fair. The village, once plain 'Buckland', was now proudly titled Buckland Monachorum, or 'Buckland of the Monks'.

Right An illuminated letter from the *Valor Ecclesiasticus*, a valuation report of the church's wealth commissioned in 1535 by Henry VIII, a year before he began the Dissolution

Troubled times

Buckland was badly hit, as were other monasteries, by the Black Death, the terrible bubonic plague that first swept the country in 1349. Lack of a labour force saw crops unharvested and tenants unable to pay their rents. Also, the balance of labour was shifting and by 1461 only the home farm was handled by the monks, with all the other granges leased and tenanted.

Life inside the abbey was changing too. Food was richer, there were more home comforts and the beautiful plain Gregorian chant practised by the first brothers had been superseded by complicated music. In May 1522 the incumbent abbot, Thomas Whyte, signed an agreement with Robert Derkeham, who, in return for organ playing and teaching, and instructing boys of the abbey to play and sing, would receive a good wage of £2 13s 4d a year. In addition he was given a comfortable room, appetising food, beer and bread, wax candles, enough wood for a decent fire and an expensive new gown each year.

Dissolution

The biggest change, and the one that spelled the end for the monasteries, came when Henry VIII, in conflict with the pope over the matter of his divorce, split from the Roman Catholic Church and appointed himself head of the Church of England. He saw the abbots as landowners who had exceeded themselves in terms of wealth and influence, and monasteries as treasure houses.

Buckland managed to avoid the first cull in 1536, when its motherhouse at Quarr was swept away. Two of Quarr's monks came to Buckland. Old Abbot Whyte was forced out by the abbey's steward, the Marquis of Exeter, who happened to be Henry's cousin. The corrupt John Toker known, according to poor old ex-Abbot Whyte, for his 'untoward conversation', was given the top job in the abbey. The cunning Toker, knowing that hard days lay ahead, set about feathering his own nest and that of his family. Toker's brother, Robert, and his two nephews were allowed to lease the tithes of the monastery churches, including that of Buckland Monachorum, while Robert retained his position as the well-paid bailiff of other abbey lands.

On 28 February 1539 Toker surrendered Buckland Abbey to the royal commissioner William Petre. Toker did rather well out of the Dissolution and his pension was set at an enormous £60 a year and he eventually became vicar of Buckland Monachorum; his monks also received reasonable pensions. However, he had sealed Buckland Abbey's fate: more than two hundred and fifty years of Cistercian occupation were ended at the stroke of a pen.

Above A 16th-century portrait of King Henry VIII

Home of the Rich and Famous

The monks were pensioned off, the abbey dissolved, but Buckland didn't have to wait long for new owners keen to establish a country seat.

The abbey transformed into a grand family home

Buckland Abbey was now the property of the Crown, for Henry VIII to do with as he pleased, and it pleased him to offer it to a loyal subject. In 1541, the abbey and about a quarter of the estate were sold for £233 3s 4d to Richard Grenville. The Grenvilles were an old Devon family, from Bideford, and Richard had served as the king's Marshall of Calais until late 1540.

The now knighted Sir Richard intended the estate for his son Roger, who moved in with his wife Thomasine and son Richard, perhaps inhabiting a monastic outbuilding. Their estate of 568 acres, renamed the Buckland Grenville estate, included all the monastic, domestic and agricultural buildings, the orchards and a long list of fields, each named on a tithe map.

However, Roger was not at Buckland long enough to establish a family home, being either at court or at sea. Roger was a gentleman of Henry VIII's Privy Chamber and distinguished himself as a captain of the royal fleet. It was a brilliant but brief career: on 19 July 1545, Roger died on board the Mary Rose during an attack on the galleys of a French invasion fleet. His son was only three years old.

Richard's inheritance

On Roger's death the estate reverted to old Sir Richard and his wife, Dame Maude. Thomasine remarried, moving with her son and new husband, Thomas Arundell, to Clifton in the parish of Landulph, about seven miles by river from Buckland. However, Richard didn't have long to wait for his inheritance: when his grandfather died in 1550, the Buckland estate was his. He was not yet eight years old.

We don't know whether work had started on converting the abbey into a house before young Richard inherited. His grandfather's will gave Dame Maude the right to fell timber for building 'the mansion place', but the elderly widow died just a few months after her husband.

An ambitious man

An⁰ · D̄NI · 1571 ·
ÆTATIS · SVÆ ·
· 29 ·

Grenville, killed

Richard's inheritance came to him young, long before he was content to settle into the genteel lifestyle of the landed gentry. When he came of age in 1563, he promptly sold land at Buckland and embarked on a life of adventure.

Before joining a group of West Country volunteers to fight in Hungary, zealously evicting Turks under the direction of the Holy Roman Emperor Maximilian, he married and moved to the family home at Stowe, leaving estate management to agents. Buckland was much lower on his list of priorities than being at the forefront of the action, and further land sales funded an expedition to Ireland where he quashed a rebellion and became Sheriff of Cork.

A strong family trait

Richard's temperament accorded with historian A. L. Rowse's observations about the Grenville family who, he said, were affected with a 'new and active strain of immense and passionate energy'. This was not always to the good, accompanied as it was by a 'harsh domineering note … betraying signs of overstrain and unbalance'. This evidenced itself in 1652 when, as a student at London's Inner Temple, Richard became embroiled in a street brawl near St Clement Danes, running his sword through Robert Bannester, a London gentleman who died of his wounds. Richard received a pardon.

The lure of Spanish gold

All the while his eyes and ears were turned across the oceans, where tales of exploration on the high seas by those two increasingly high-profile sailors, Francis Drake and John Hawkins, were firing public imagination. By 1571 Richard, now a Member of Parliament, was planning his own voyage in his ship *The Castle of Comfort*, hoping to claim new lands south and west of the Americas and bring home Spanish gold. In 1574 he and a group of adventurers petitioned the Queen for a licence '... for discovery of sundry rich and unknown lands ... reserved for England, and for the honour of your Majesty'. However, the Queen prevaricated and by late 1574 she withdrew the licence.

Richard's retirement

It might have been this full stop to his privateering ambitions that saw him at last return to Buckland to build a family home. Of the many substantial buildings still standing at Buckland, Richard chose the most unlikely for his conversion. The abbey church occupied a good-sized space. In the centre of that space, at the church crossing, directly underneath the tower, he built his Great Hall. The high walls of the chancel and nave accommodated two more floors, each split into substantial rooms.

Left Sir Richard Grenville after an unknown artist, 17th century based on a work of 1571

Right The south side of the tower where Sir Richard sited his Great Hall

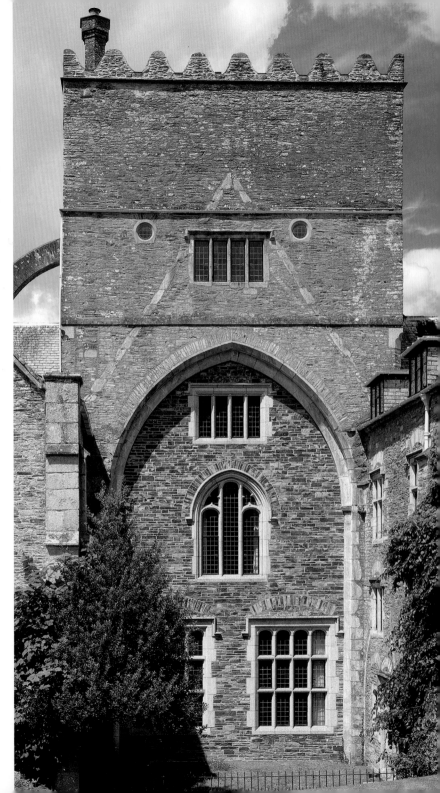

Sir Richard's domestic designs

Sir Richard's bold conversion is evident today, although the shape of the house and its surrounding buildings changed two centuries later, when architect Samuel Pepys Cockerell remodelled the structure.

We don't know the exact arrangement of the living space in Sir Richard's new home but he lived here for four years, presumably with his wife, Mary St Leger, and six children. Parish records show that his daughter, Bridget, was christened at Buckland Monachorum in 1578.

His dramatic decision to demolish the south transept of the church allowed daylight to flood into the Great Hall. Visitors today can see, quite clearly, the roofline of the old transept on the southern face of the tower. A screens passage to the east of the Great Hall allowed access to the Grenville family's up-to-the-moment kitchen wing, the large kitchen fitted with an enormous open hearth, the chimney breast supported by a granite lintel under a brick archway. The hearth on the west wall, constructed after Sir Richard's time, has two bread ovens.

Below The outline of the demolished south transept

They were bricked up at some point in the 18th century and a row of then-fashionable brick charcoal 'stewing stoves' fitted in their place. Many small rooms around the kitchen served as stores or chambers for the senior staff such as housekeepers and butlers.

Writing on the wall

So did all these domestic improvements mean Sir Richard had hung up his sword and shield and opted for a quiet retirement in the country? A section of the fine plaster frieze in Richard's Great Hall seems to suggest as much. Skulls, intimations of mortality, peep from hourglasses set below a great tangled vine upon which a weary soldier, divested of his armour, has hung his shield. Nearby, jumbled in a heap on the ground beside his warhorse who has been turned loose to rest, are his weapons.

The next section of the frieze, over the fireplace, dated 1576, is a far more conventional representation of those sensible figures: Justice with her scales, Temperance watering the wine, Fortitude bravely suffering the embrace of a snake, and Prudence bearing the Bible. Above these good women are three magnificent hoofed and bearded satyrs, bearing shields and decorating the curved ceiling trusses.

While Richard's overseas adventuring may have been on hold, he remained something of a firebrand and his four years at Buckland saw him zealously carrying out his role as Sheriff of Cornwall and head of the judiciary, hunting Catholic recusants for the government and seeing them hanged. He was knighted for these 'services' in October 1577.

Top right The 16th-century
kitchen built by
Sir Richard

Bottom right Sir Richard's
Great Hall

Sir Richard sets sail once more

Why did Sir Richard, settled into the life of a country gentleman, respected by his peers and trusted by the government, decide to sell his house and estate in order to once more seek a life of danger and adventure?

Nearing forty, Sir Richard put Buckland Grenville on the market at the end of 1580. It may be that he was short of money or felt a longing for the old family home at Stowe in Cornwall. Perhaps the plaster pictures in his Great Hall at Buckland reminded him of the life from which he had retired. Or perhaps he could not contain his jealousy of master mariner Francis Drake, newly returned from his voyage around the world. Even more galling was that Drake had brought back untold wealth, his ship ballasted with Spanish silver and gold, taken as he plundered the west coast of Spanish America – the very voyage that Sir Richard had petitioned for, but had been forbidden to make, a few years earlier.

We don't know if Sir Richard harboured animosity towards his popular contemporary, but it is likely, especially as Drake's was a yeoman family of no consequence in the eyes of a proud Grenville. Drake's daring exploits, his success as a slaver, a relentless pirate and thorn in the flesh of the wealthy Spanish made him the darling of the moment and favourite of the Queen.

Sir Richard Grenvill K.t

Right An ageing Sir Richard gave up his retirement to return to the high seas

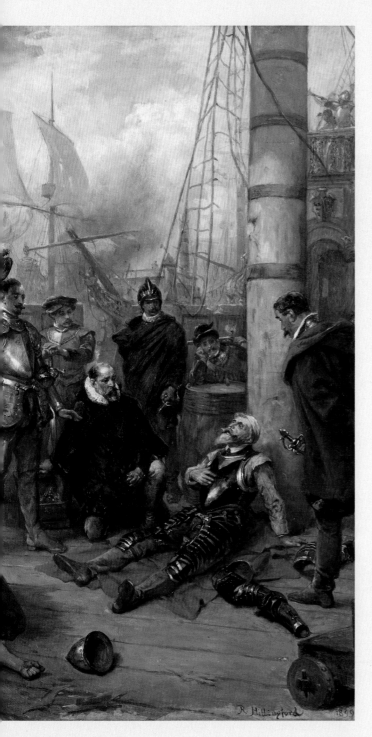

Sir Richard's last adventure

Sir Richard died at sea in 1591, when, disobeying his admiral's orders to retreat, he recklessly sailed his ship *The Revenge* into the heart of a far superior Spanish force at Flores. Sir Richard was shot, most of his crew died, and his ship was pounded to splinters.

Alfred Tennyson's poem 'The Revenge: A Ballad of the Fleet' made him the hero of the day, but those who knew him as an intolerably proud and ambitious man, thought his actions wilful and obstinate.

He had only a hundred seamen to work the ship and to
  fight,
And he sail'd away from Flores till the Spaniard came in
  sight,
With his huge sea-castles heaving upon the weather bow.
'Shall we fight or shall we fly?
Good Sir Richard, tell us now,
For to fight is but to die!
There'll be little of us left by the time this sun be set.'
And Sir Richard said again: 'We be all good English men,
Let us bang these dogs of Seville, the children of the devil,
For I never turned my back on Don or devil yet.'

* * *

And the stately Spanish men to their flagship bore him
  then,
Where they laid him by the mast, old Sir Richard caught at
  last,
And they praised him to his face with their courtly foreign
  grace.
But he rose upon their decks and he cried:
'I have fought for Queen and Faith like a valiant man and
  true;
I have only done my duty as a man is bound to do:
With a joyful spirit I Sir Richard Grenville die!'
And he fell upon their decks and he died.

Bought by the nation's darling

It is 26 September 1580 and the people of Plymouth are buzzing with excitement. A small galleon, spotted sailing up Plymouth Sound, now lies at anchor off St Nicholas Island. This can mean only one thing: Drake is home.

When Francis Drake set sail on a December day three years earlier to circumnavigate the globe, plundering Spanish treasure ships on the way, he did so with the support of Queen Elizabeth, smarting from the 'divers injuries that we have received' from the King of Spain. But Drake knew that political climates changed and that Elizabeth and King Philip of Spain, whose ships he had relieved of hundreds of thousands of pounds' worth of gold and silver, might now be the best of friends. So he is pacing the deck of the treasure-filled *Golden Hind*, waiting for word from his wife, Mary, that it is safe to come ashore.

He need not have worried. A delighted Elizabeth summoned him to London where he was accorded a hero's welcome. In the spring of 1581, at Deptford, she dined with him on the *Golden Hind* and awarded him a knighthood, doubtless mindful of the £160,000 that was her share of the booty, more than enough to run the government of England for a whole year. She privately told him to take £10,000, a vast sum of wealth in the late 16th century, and to allow an equal amount to be shared between his crew.

The Drakes come to Buckland

Elizabeth I's very public praise, reinforced by the knighthood, was intended not only to thank Drake, but also as a pointed insult to King Philip of Spain, whose ships had been attacked by the man he regarded as the worst of English pirates.

Drake, now extremely wealthy, asked his friend Christopher Harris of Plymstock to take care of his share of the treasure. Very soon Harris and another businessman, John Hele, approached Sir Richard Grenville's agents in pursuit of the purchase of Buckland Abbey.

Acting on Drake's behalf, they agreed to pay £3,400 for the house, its contents and 202 hectares (500 acres) of land, with the proviso that Sir Richard would buy the house back after three years if Drake no longer wanted it.

Drake, who became Mayor of Plymouth in 1581, was living with his wife, Mary Newman, in a large house in the city's Looe Street, before moving to Buckland, probably in 1582. The couple had no children of their own, but brought up Mary's orphaned nephew, Jonas, Drake's younger brother Thomas and his cousin, John.

Far left Queen Elizabeth knights Francis Drake on board his ship, the *Golden Hind* at Deptford, after his voyage round the world

Left Sir Francis Drake by Marcus Gheeraerts the younger

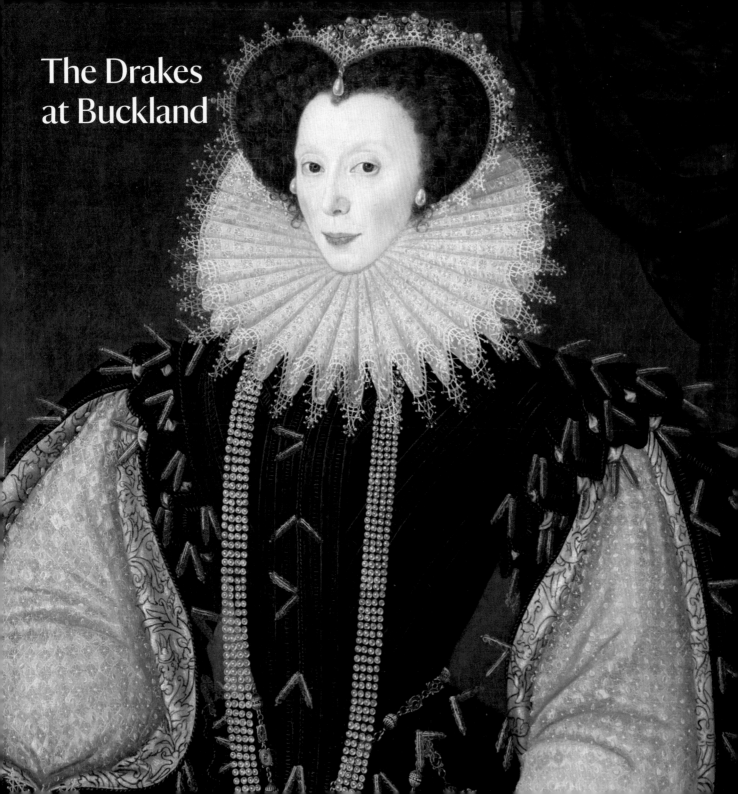

The Drakes
at Buckland

Lady Mary did not live long enough to enjoy Buckland. She died in the couple's town house in January 1583, receiving not one, but two funeral services. The first was at St Andrews Church in Plymouth, the second a burial at nearby parish church of St Budeaux, where she and Francis had married in 1569.

Mary's death came at a difficult time for Drake, land-bound after many years at sea. Now rich and famous, he was courted by local officials and businessmen, and for several years his preoccupation was his homeport of Plymouth. He served as a councillor and mayor, overseeing the town's defences and bringing, largely at his own expense, a new water supply by way of an aqueduct from the River Meavy on Dartmoor. At the same time he proved a canny businessman. He bought not only Buckland Abbey, but also many properties in Plymouth and manors in the countryside.

Drake makes his mark

But it was Buckland that he chose for his own home, perhaps because of its river links with the wider seas at Plymouth, and perhaps because he sought some peace away from the turmoil of battle and long debates in the council chamber. So it was to Buckland, not long after Mary's death, that he brought home a new bride, the beautiful and well-connected Elizabeth Sydenham.

Drake seems not to have made alterations to the house that Grenville built, although his coat of arms, granted by Queen Elizabeth after his circumnavigation of the globe, are seen above a fireplace in an upstairs gallery. Downstairs, in the kitchen, hang the antlers of a deer said to have frightened the brave captain more than an encounter with Spanish raiders. Legend says that Drake took refuge in an oak tree, climbing down to shoot the deer only as it trotted away.

Left The second Lady Drake, Elizabeth Sydenham, by George Gower

Above The coat of arms of Buckland Abbey's most famous resident, Sir Francis Drake – 'Great things from small beginnings'

Buckland's swashbuckling hero

Sir Richard was seemingly restless during his time at Buckland and his successor similarly so. While Drake enjoyed Buckland, playing the country gentleman, county official and fond husband, he was on standby, waiting for a call for his services.

It came in 1585 when Elizabeth, stung by reports of Spanish plans for a naval invasion, ordered him back to sea with a fleet of 21 ships. He sailed for Spain, attacking Vigo before raiding Spanish possessions in Europe and then across the Atlantic in America. To the Spanish he was the very devil, an evil pirate. They called him El Draque ('The Dragon'). Twenty thousand ducats was the price put on his head by King Philip II.

Skirmishes with the Spanish

He wasn't home for long before another call came, to 'singe the beard of the King of Spain'. Drake was summoned to attack the heart of the Spanish fleet. His daring raids on Cadiz and Corunna harbours, destroying almost 40 ships, delayed the deployment of the Armada for a year.

But Phillip was not put off. In 1588, the following year, 130 Spanish ships formed an invasion force to overthrow Queen Elizabeth. The English fleet, under Lord Howard and Drake, pursued the Armada as they tried to anchor in the Solent. As Drake broke away and captured the galleon Rosario, the Spanish finally dropped anchor off Calais, where they were scattered by Drake's fireships. The ensuing battle saw the

Left The defeat of the Spanish Armada, 1588

Spaniards driven by gales up the east coast of England, harried by the lighter English ships. Many foundered on the rocky coastline, while terrible storms in the Atlantic on the return to Spain wrought more damage.

Drake defiant to the end

Drake was again the hero. However, the tables were turned just 12 months later when he and Sir John Norreys led a 'counter-Armada' to destroy what remained of the Spanish fleet. The expedition was unsuccessful, with the loss of thousands of English lives and 20 ships.

By the time he was 50 Drake had the appearance of an old man. Marcus Gheeraerts' portrait of him, made around 1590, shows a lined, sunken face. In 1595 he led his last expedition with his old friend and relative, John Hawkins, to the West Indies. It was a disaster. The Spanish fleet repelled the English attack. Hawkins died off San Juan de Puerto Rico and Drake, succumbing to the dysentery that took so many of his crew, breathed his last on 27 January 1596 on board *The Defiance*.

His sorrowful men dressed their leader in full armour, placing his body in a coffin of lead, wrapped in the flag of St George. Blasts from English guns and cannons thundered across the sea to Puerto Bello as the coffin slipped under the waves and Francis Drake, the swashbuckling hero of so many battles, went to his rest in foreign waters.

Right This portrait of Sir Francis Drake by Marcus Gheeraerts shows an aged mariner

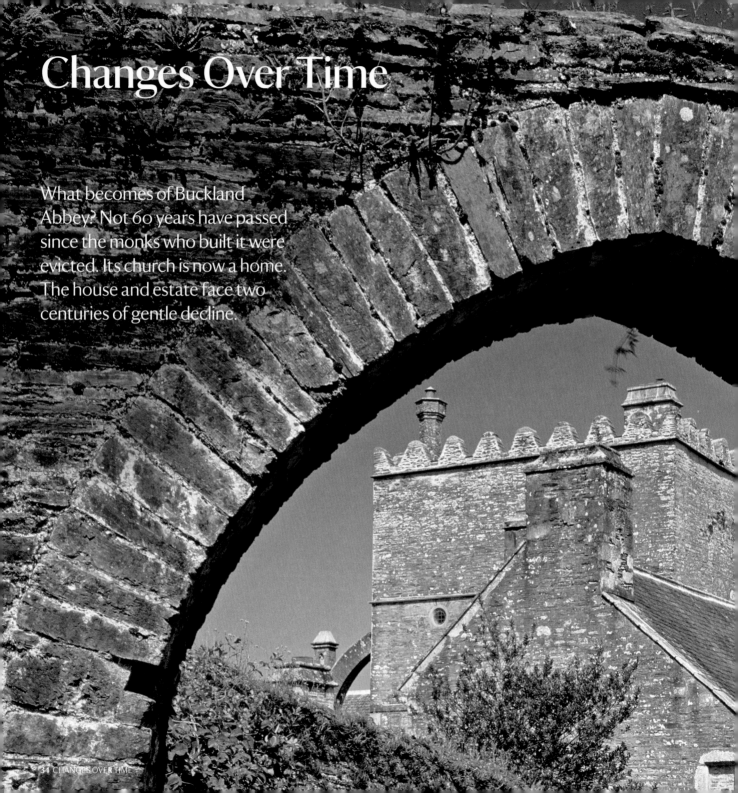

Changes Over Time

What becomes of Buckland
Abbey? Not 60 years have passed
since the monks who built it were
evicted. Its church is now a home.
The house and estate face two
centuries of gentle decline.

Drake had no descendants. His marriages were childless. He left Buckland's contents to his widow, Elizabeth Sydenham (apart from a gold cup and plate set aside to be sold to pay off any debts), but the house and the rest of his property went to his brother, Thomas. Elizabeth was permitted to live in the house until her death. We know little of Elizabeth, who was almost 20 years younger than Drake. She re-married soon after, to Sir William Courtenay of Powderham. Elizabeth died in 1598 in her late thirties.

Buckland was occupied by Drakes for some time, however when opposition to Charles I increased in the late 1630s, the Drakes made the mistake of supporting the Parliamentarians. This was dangerous in Royalist Devon. The Sir Francis Drake of the time was booted out and the Buckland estate granted to King Charles' general in the west, Richard 'Skellum' Grenville ('skellum' was local slang for a rogue or rascal).

Buckland restored

Buckland was restored to Sir Francis and Lady Drake by 1646 – complete with a new riding school built by Skellum. A 1660s inventory at the Restoration, when the Drakes were pardoned by the King, showed a diminished estate of 277 acres, a small mill, four orchards, woods, two gardens, hop yards and nurseries.

A 1680 inventory of estate livestock lists two bulls, large cows and heifers and young cattle, oxen and calves, ewes and lambs, 'weathers' (wethers or neutered rams), young sheep and rams, one coach and horses, riding and 'labour' horses, mares and colts, 'hoggs' and 'two pairs of great wheelers'.

Left Buckland Abbey's buildings are much changed yet keep their ancient character

Estate details

At the end of the 17th century and up to her death in 1717, Elizabeth Drake, the third wife of yet another Sir Francis, left us a glimpse into a busy farming household in her account books.

Over the years the books show payments for an estate manager, several gardeners, a shepherd, and 'Anne Rodeman and her daughter' for 'beating ye peasefield'. Income is recorded for sales of salmon, honey, wood, thatching reed,

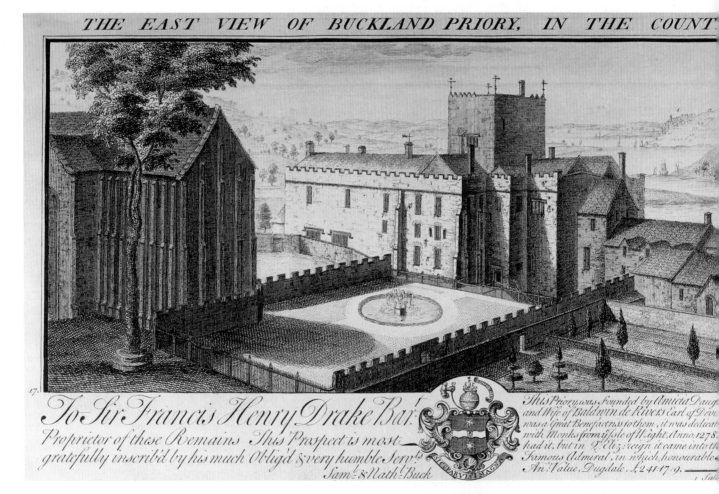

THE EAST VIEW OF BUCKLAND PRIORY, IN THE COUNT

To Sir Francis Henry Drake Bar.
Proprietor of these Remains This Prospect is most gratefully inscrib'd by his much Oblig'd & very humble Serv.ts Sam.l & Nath.l Buck

This Priory, was Founded by Amicia Daug. and Wife of Baldwin de Rivers Earl of Dev. was a Great Benefactriss to them, it was dedicat with Monks from ysle of Wight, Anno.1278 had it, but in Q. Eliz. reign it came into the Famous Admiral, in which, honourable An. Value, Dugdale. £241-17-9.

fish, cherries, 'pairs', 'plumbs', 'cowcumbers', onions, walnuts, roses, 'rasburys' and 'peale' (sea trouts'). Also sold were 'heartichokes, half a score Fat Yows, cider and a seam (cart load) of apples'. Payments out included cash for hinges for the pulpit door, 'canvis' for coach windows, rat-catching, locks for the apple store and pigeon house, seeds, nails and a thousand cabbage plants.

However, the closing of Elizabeth's meticulously kept account books on her death in 1717 saw the beginning of Buckland's decline, hastened by her son's inheritance of another country house.

'This decay'd Place'

Elizabeth's old family home, Nutwell Court at Exmouth, passed to her son, Francis Henry, in 1732. By the middle of the century his son, another Francis Henry, the 5th Baronet, made Nutwell his principal residence, leaving Buckland to the care of his mother, the dowager Lady Anne Drake. Buckland began, literally, to fall to pieces.

The picture of decay is painted eloquently in letters written by Nicholas Rowe, Sir Francis' steward. Rowe, doing his best to keep the cherry

brandy and cider-making business going at Buckland, sent reports to Francis Henry of new trees planted in the orchards and gardens. But his despair at the state of the house and gardens is evident. In May 1753 he writes: 'For my part this place is a sinker ... as to this decay'd Place, I don't see what can be Done to it, but cutting weed etc – the House! Oh the House! What can be Done to That?' Later, he writes: '... poor Buckland! I fear they won't make a Pipe of Cyder this Season. Your Mama's hine [farm manager] is much out of order. But some Cherrys are left & I've sent to Mrs Porter for some Brandy ... and I've put some Fresh Fruit to it.'

'It rains in all the rooms'

The state of the house is even worse the following year – the only cheering news was that of a good yield of cider. In mid-December 1754 Rowe writes: 'To see this place makes me Lower, if possible than before, it rains in all the rooms in the house, part of the ceiling in the room you Dine in is fallen Down, the gardens look wild ... the pears you ordered to be Sav'd rotted away so fast [we] could not Save Them.' However, he was able to report: '2–300 Hogsheads of Cyder this week'.

Below The East View of Buckland Priory, Devon, 1734, by Samuel and Nathaniel Buck

A rich record during a time of decline
The 18th-century appearance of Buckland Abbey is beautifully illustrated in an engraving made in 1734 by the Buck Brothers (see left). Samuel and Nathaniel Buck, printmakers and engravers, made their names with a series of engravings of ancient castles and monastic buildings, known as 'Bucks' Antiquities'. Their fine engraving of Buckland Abbey shows formal walled Tudor gardens, Grenville's east wing, the crossing tower and the original north transept of the abbey. It also gives clues as to the layout of the 13th-century abbey buildings. What were probably the abbey cloisters and their associated buildings such as the chapter house are shown to the north of the church. It is thought these were demolished at the beginning of the 19th century.

Georgian restoration

After the death of Lady Anne Drake in 1768, Sir Francis Henry decided to take Buckland back in hand and ordered the modernisation and panelling of the rooms in the east wing.

Another of Sir Francis Henry's additions is the beautifully crafted staircase that rises through four floors. An oak gate was fixed to discourage dogs from scampering up these fine stairs.

More work was needed but nothing more changed until after his death in 1794, when two modernising characters helped the new owner, Francis Augustus Elliott, Lord Heathfield, restore the house and the estate.

Cockerell and Marshall

Samuel Pepys Cockerell, a fashionable London architect (and the great-great nephew of the famous diarist) was charged with 'fitting up' the house for 'occasional residence'. By 1801, when he started supervising his new designs, another reformer was already hard at work, transforming the neglected estate into what was to become a model farm.

William Marshall, an enlightened agricultural economist, had been called in by Sir Francis Henry in 1791 to assess the condition of the estate. Marshall, horrified at its 'disgraceful state', but recognising the potential for improvement, based himself at Buckland Place, as he called it, over the following years.

His first view, in July 1791 was not encouraging: 'The situation is naturally recluse, and is now rendered truly so, by long neglect.' He acknowledges, however, the beauty of the river-fed landscape with its tree-clad hillsides: 'The irregularly winding estuaries and the rapid torrents ... and the wild coppices that hang on the sides of its hills ... exhibit scenery of the most romantic and picturesque…. When the meadows of Buckland, and the meek grounds of Maristow (a country house beside the Tavy) blend their lawny surfaces with the wood and water, scenes the most delightful are formed.'

Care of cabbages

Like Nicholas Rowe, the long-departed farm steward, Marshall despaired at the management regime of the 'hines' or farm managers. He writes that the 'present degeneracy' of the Buckland cattle herd had come about because of poor care. Only one farming practice met with his approval: 'the only useful idea I have been able to collect, from the late manager of this farm, is his method of cutting garden Cabbages ... he cuts the body of the Cabbage only ... the consequence is a second, and perhaps a third crop of Cabbages'.

Marshall's measures

Three years into his study at Buckland, Marshall put together a plan to initiate change. In 1794, the year that Sir Francis Henry, the man he regarded as a friend, died, he started, cautiously, to make improvements.

He advocated sheep farming as the estate's primary activity – just as Abbot Robert and his monks had, five hundred years earlier. Turnips, barley and wheat should be grown while dairy cattle should be a secondary line.

From the days of the monks, the production and sale of cider had been a feature of life on the estate. Marshall was quick to admire the cider rooms, putting them among the best in the country, and he praised the practice of mulching the roots of the trees with a strip of sward. But he condemned at least thirty acres of the orchards themselves, planted in water meadows or facing the bleak north. He wasn't too keen either on the effects of cider itself on the locals; 'Their Orchards might well be styled their Temples, and Apple Trees their idols of Worship,' he noted sardonically.

Right This cider press in the Great Barn is an example of the sort that would have been used at Buckland

Out with the old

He was scathing about the state of the pasture, instigating a new programme of ploughing, harrowing, rolling, manuring and fallowing, while he planted new hedges of blackthorn and bushy shrubs and constructed new weirs in the fishery to prevent erosion of the banks of the Tavy.

An ancient rill, built to bring water to meadowland, was admired. Conjecturing that 'this was introduced under the auspices of the Church', he acknowledged the monks' expertise in water management, before designing a new system of hillside gutters from a small stream to keep most of the meadowland well watered. Perhaps the most significant of his changes are those to the farm buildings. While Marshall greatly admired the magnificent tithe barn, he altered its layout to suit his new management system, cutting new doors to allow the great space to be divided into six bays and to allow wagons to be driven inside. He proceeded to make the farmyard a compact unit, observing that the scattered buildings and the steepness of the slope, made for an 'awkward' layout.

Above The Great Barn painted in 1831 by John White Abbot; two farm workers are seen going about their business

Farmyard design

Marshall's rearrangement of the farmyard included constructing the Ox Yard, the semi-octagonal area outside today's shop and restaurant. The cattle sheds, which housed the ploughing teams of oxen, are now craft workshops. An impressive black ox, sculpted in steel by Jonathan Rodney-Jones in 2000, stands guard.

The shop and restaurant occupy an early 14th-century building known as the 'Monks' Guesthouse' although it was probably originally a row of stables underneath a large hayloft. It was Sir Richard Grenville who had it converted into a guesthouse, long after the monks had departed. He had his arms and those of the St Legers, his wife's family, fixed above the south windows.

The cattle, their fodder stores and the dung yard in front of the stalls were brought together in close proximity to the heart of the farmyard, the great barn. Another cattle shed or traditional Devon 'linhay' lies to the left of the Ox Yard, opposite the barn, while nearby was the milking yard, two straw yards and more cowsheds and stables. Marshall was thorough, ensuring the stalls were slightly sloped so that all the run-off went straight to the dung pit, all pillars were fixed onto moorland granite blocks to prevent decay, while internal walls were buttressed against pressure from the raised roadways outside.

It is likely that the demolition of the north transept of the church, the cloisters and their attendant buildings, shown in the Buck engraving of 1734, happened at this time.

Marshalling the workforce

Under Marshall's regime, almost thirty men, women and apprentices, a dozen oxen and six horses were hard at work on the land. The men drove the oxen ploughing the fields while the horse teams prepared the ground by harrowing and rolling. Marshall wrote of ploughing: 'I have never seen so much cheerfulness attending the operation of plowing, anywhere, as in Devonshire.'

The men also moved wood, made hay, spread muck and mowed. Others looked after the sheep and cattle, while everyone came together for the seasonal jobs of sowing, harvesting and fixing the hedges and fences. The women weeded the garden and 'turneps', picked stones, hoed the carrots and picked apples.

Opposite A mid-20th-century aerial view shows the arrangements of Marshall's design

Below Buckland's two-storeyed linhay

Keeping the character

Above Cockerell was at pains to keep and incorporate features that gave the abbey its medieval character

Cockerell's bill came to more than £7,000. He understood the historic importance of the abbey, insisting in an early 'Particulars of Works' that 'no alteration must be attempted to the character of the building'.

Cockerell designed a mock-transept to enclose the 'spacious and cheerful access', which featured a new front door and staircase. The latter was destroyed by fire in 1938 (see pages 47 and 48). Today's staircase is utilitarian rather than elegant, hardly surprising given that the destruction happened at a time when the country was at war and other matters were more pressing.

Toned-down tributes

Poor Cockerell had to scale down his plans for an elaborate tribute to Sir Francis Drake in an earlier design for this entrance, featuring a 'sea-walk and memorial'. He went so far as to exhibit drawings for the walk at the Royal Academy in 1801 but they were turned down for a more sober Gothic approach. However a later visitor, Rachel Evans, who came to Buckland in 1846, describes a shady walk under enormous cedar trees where, in the recesses of the paths, were 'ancient figures' carved from wood, some defaced but others, covered with moss and lichen, clearly representing Neptunes and Tritons. She deduced they were intended 'to honour the great mariner', so maybe Cockerell's walk was built after all, in another place.

Some significant losses

By whose orders, Cockerell or Marshall, the demolition of the old monastic buildings to the north of the abbey was undertaken is not known, but it is thought they were removed at this time. Estate accounts for the two years from 1800 show much labour and time spent on carting stones, cob and rubble away as well as bringing in new sand, bricks, stones and timbers.

The Fuller-Elliott-Drakes

Enticing rental particulars were released in 1815 on the orders of Buckland's new owner, Thomas Trayton-Fuller, Lord Heathfield's nephew. Trayton-Fuller, who changed his name to Elliott-Drake, decided Buckland was

'well-furnished and fit for immediate reception of a family of distinction'. Like his uncle, Elliott-Drake preferred to live at Nutwell Court.

Cockerell's renovation had ensured three sitting rooms, seven best bedchambers, five dressing rooms plus servants' quarters, plenty of stabling for horses and three coach houses. It must have been comfortable and convenient, for there was no shortage of families of distinction eager to become tenants throughout the 18th century.

By now the Drake blood was thinly dispersed through the veins of nieces and nephews but, in 1902, the family returned to Buckland when the grandly named Sir Francis George Augustus Fuller-Elliott-Drake and his wife, Elizabeth, took up residence.

Above Buckland Abbey, Devonshire, the seat of T. T. F. Drake, Esq. an engraving by Henry Wallis after S. Condy of 1833, after Cockerell's remodellings

Times of great change

Elizabeth, the last Lady Drake, became a very grand mistress of the house when she and her husband moved to Buckland, where she published a scholarly account of the Drake family history dating back to the master mariner.

Her carriage, drawn by a matching pair of black horses, would convey her to the market town of Yelverton, two footmen in their dark green and white livery riding on the box. The shopkeepers would be expected to come outside to her ladyship's carriage door, solicitously enquiring after the health of the Drake family, before attending to her needs.

A new place of worship

Lady Drake's daughter, another Elizabeth, inherited when her father died in 1915 and, although she and her husband, Lord Seaton, took care to endow the village with amenities such as a playing field and a men's club, they lived quietly, working on restoring the abbey.

It was Elizabeth Seaton who, when the site of the high altar of the monks was uncovered during repair work in 1917, turned the room, once a servants' hall, into a Roman Catholic chapel. It was re-dedicated to St Benedict and the Blessed Virgin Mary. A new altar was made where once the monks had knelt, two small ribbed vaults reconstructed beneath traceried arches and the original piscina, the basin used for washing holy vessels, discovered and restored. The mystery of empty graves below the altar has teased historians for one hundred years. An annual mass is still celebrated in the chapel.

A family treasure

The Drake Jewel, an elaborate gold locket, decorated with pearls, diamonds and rubies, given to Sir Francis by Queen Elizabeth, became a treasured family possession. It is now part of a private collection but it can be seen being worn by Sir Francis in the Marcus Gheeraerts painting (see page 29), while his second wife, Elizabeth Sydenham, has it pinned at the waist, in a portrait made after her marriage. Another family member, Elizabeth, Lady Seaton, wears it attached to a string of pearls in a portrait painted by Edwin Long in 1884 (see left).

Above A 15th-century alabaster carving of the Virgin of the Annunciation

Right Carved stones from the original Tudor chapel reredos, placed beneath the altar table in the chapel

Left Elizabeth Beatrice Drake, Lady Seaton, by Edwin Long

Buckland Abbey ablaze

Another era draws to a close. Lady Seaton, widowed, died in 1937 as drums of war began to beat over a troubled Europe. The last Drake (the one with the longest name), Captain Richard Owen-Tapps-Gervaise-Meyrick, inherited and moved in. He, his wife and two sons, had been here for less than a year when, on a cold January morning, a maid rushed into the kitchen shouting that a chimney was on fire. The blaze spread with horrible speed until the flames threatened the whole of the west wing, once the nave of the old abbey church.

Rescued for the nation

The alarm was raised; all hands, family and staff hurried to save priceless Drake treasures, precious furniture and paintings, while firemen worked tirelessly to douse the blaze which broke out time and again as the roof of the old building collapsed.

Britain was at war by the time the repairs were completed in 1940. New fireproof floors and a steel-truss roof were put in place. Sir Richard Grenville's horizontal division of the abbey's nave in the late 16th century made a first-floor space that was divided into bedrooms and dressing rooms. The floor was rebuilt without reinstating all these divisions and left mostly open.

In 1946 Buckland Abbey and the surrounding land, including Lopwell Quay and the home farm, were advertised for sale. After more than

HISTORIC BUCKLAND ABBEY ABLAZE

350 years in the possession of the Drake family, the ancient abbey house – the burial place of monks, the home of brave seafarers, a peaceful retreat tucked deep in the Devonshire countryside – was to be sold at public auction. Neighbours and locals held their breath while its future hung in the balance. The abbey and estate were bought privately, before the day set for auction, by a Yelverton landowner, Captain Arthur Rodd. Without delay he presented the abbey, its garden, driveway and lodge to the National Trust.

Preparations for the public

The gift, welcome as it was, came with a list of extensive and expensive repairs. Death-watch beetle ticked away in the woodwork, and the derelict stairs in the west wing had to be replaced. Plymouth City Council joined forces with the National Trust and took responsibility for the repair work. The aim at that time was to convert the abbey into a museum to showcase the life of Sir Francis Drake and the naval and social history of the West Country.

As repair work progressed, glimpses of the monastic stonework were revealed, showing the earlier, more austere time in the abbey's life. Carved stone corbels, the 'springers' (the lowest stone in a vaulted archway), a short length of mullion, or cornice were brought to view as the plaster that had buried them for centuries was scraped away.

In 1951, at the height of the Festival of Britain celebrations, the doors of the abbey opened to a public eager to visit this house that had so many fascinating associations with so much of our country's history.

Opposite From the newspaper story reporting the fire at Buckland Abbey

Right Painstakingly restored stonework original to the medieval abbey

Completing the picture

Thirty years later, the National Trust, having bought a further 280 hectares (700 acres) of the original estate, took over management of the abbey. On 19 July 1988, exactly 400 years after the Armada was sighted off the English coast, Buckland Abbey, with a new visitor centre, shop and restaurant, re-opened after a year-long refurbishment.

The last pieces of the jigsaw were fitted in 2011 when the Cider House and Tower Cottage were acquired.

Visitors experience more than seven centuries of history as they explore the abbey. A room fitted out in elegant Georgian style at the turn of the 18th and 19th centuries has an ancient reminder of the 13th-century monastic church. High up in one corner, the winged ox of St Luke, carved as a stone corbel, breaks through the plaster, supporting a small section of what was once a soaring arch, helping to hold the great vaulted roof of the church nave in place. In a passageway, the eagle of St John, once part of the same vaulting, is similarly exposed, the carving still sharp and clear.

Above Tower Cottage was acquired by the Trust in 2011

Phases of history

The gallery that runs the whole length of the old nave, rebuilt after the 1938 fire, now uses steel trusses and fireproof material. But some stonework survives, a clue to the beauty and strength of the medieval vaulting.

When Grenville fitted floors across the length and width of the church nave in the 1570s, this upper storey, referred to later as 'The Great Roof' by architect Cockerell, had no divisions. It was a typical Tudor long gallery for indoor exercise on wet days. Georgian owners fitted bedrooms, a laundry and, later, a chapel. The granite fireplace built into the north crossing arch bears the Drake coat of arms. A second coat of arms, also belonging to the Drakes, is dated 1655 with the initials 'RN'. The identity of 'RN' is a mystery.

Presiding over the phase of Buckland's history that saw it occupied by Sir Francis Drake is his monumental statue. Impressive in size and pose, this giant was discovered, discarded, on a north Devon hillside. It was the working model of Sir Joseph Boehm, the sculptor responsible for large bronzes of Drake at Tavistock and Exeter.

Left A stone corbel carved with a winged ox of St Luke, uncovered and typical of the decoration that once adorned the Cistercian abbey

A celebratory ceiling

The ceiling of the room known as the Drake Chamber had a steel joist fitted after the damage caused by the fire in 1938. Sixty years later, a beautiful new ceiling, designed by Jane Schofield and hand-modelled, using lime plaster, covered the unsightly joist. Motifs appropriate to the abbey's history such as bees, fruit, shells, anchors and rope are incorporated into the design.

As Tranquil Today

The estate and the gardens around the abbey
are as much part of its story as the building itself.
Today there is plenty for visitors to explore.

Buckland Abbey's surroundings are much as they were when the Cistercians arrived over seven centuries ago. The secluded valley, with winding water, fertile meadows, a gentle climate and tree-clad slopes, offers the same peace and tranquillity that delighted the travel-weary monks when they gazed down at their new home in 1278. On the hilltops you can enjoy views of the abbey and picture the scene in the 13th century, when the ecclesiastical buildings were intact and the conversi were busy in the dairy and the forge, the brew house and bakery. Their estate, although diminished, still supports agriculture; sheep graze on the slopes near the abbey, while the orchard and kitchen garden are still productive.

Local produce

More than two acres of land close to the abbey are tended by local families, who look after bees, chickens, pigs and sheep while producing fruit and vegetables on the community allotments. There is a long tradition of cider-making at the abbey; tonnes of apples from Buckland's orchard are pressed in the Great Barn each year to give hundreds of litres of juice to turn into cider and apple juice. The fields and orchard are situated near the start of the estate trails.

Natural beauty and history

An idea of the nature of the land can be had from three trails, each designed to not only show the beauty of the landscape and the wide views from the heights of the Tavy Valley, but also to provide opportunities for watching wildlife and bird-spotting. Shy deer hide among the trees as buzzards wheel overhead, while smaller birds inhabit the woods and grassy walks.

Left The abbey, its buildings and gardens offer so much to be explored

In spring the sunlight, filtering through the branches, splashes gold onto the rich tapestry of massed bluebells. Long summer days see stately spires of deep pink foxgloves lining the paths, each plant quivering as bees probe the flowers. Autumn brings shorter days when the leaves of deciduous trees and shrubs blaze butter-yellow, vermillion, orange, deep purple and red before slowly falling to carpet the ancient paths winding down through the woods to the River Tavy. Here the monks made their weirs, trapped fish and harnessed the river's energy to turn mill wheels.

Right Cott Lane is the route the monks would have taken to and from the river

The abbey's gardens

While all traces of any domestic Tudor gardens at Buckland have disappeared, Lady Elizabeth Drake's account books of the early 18th century give us a clue about her garden during the early Georgian period.

She mentions her two full-time gardeners and, intriguingly, 'ye Ffrench Gardiner' who, in 1709, was well paid. We can only speculate that it might have been this Frenchman who designed the walled garden, beyond the north face of the Great Barn, shown in the Buck engraving of 1734 (see pages 36–37). Between the walled garden and barn is what appears to be a formal lawned area, enclosed and raised, with gravel walks around a circular pond and fountain.

The sunny west-facing front of the Great Barn is an ideal spot for the herb garden, containing plants with culinary and medicinal properties, many of which would have been familiar not only to the Grenville and Drake households, but also to the Cistercian monks. The herb garden is fragrant for much of the year with scent from thyme, rosemary, comfrey and feverfew, calamint, nepeta, fennel and artemesia.

Right **The garden beside the Great Barn**

A 20th-century design

Most of what is seen today is the work of 20th-century designers. Eminent gardeners including Vita Sackville-West and Graham Stuart Thomas were called in for advice. Many overgrown trees were taken out and replaced by acid-loving shrubs, such as camellias and azaleas, and specimen trees including eucryphia and Japanese maples. Standing on the south side of the abbey is a magnificent large evergreen magnolia, which flowers right through until the first frosts.

Behind the abbey is a level area of grass laid by Lord and Lady Seaton for use as a croquet lawn. The garden to the north, designed at the very end of the 20th century, is inspired by Tudor plantings and walks. Working with the hilly nature of the site the garden, on three levels, comprises an area enclosed by walls and trellis, with beds planted with various roses. It is backed by a small orchard from which steps rise to a peaceful grassy area.

On the way to the Cider House garden is a productive and colourful walled kitchen garden with a glasshouse, vegetable beds, a small wild-flower meadow and beds full of bright annuals and perennials. The Cider House garden leads you peacefully and prettily to a sheltered wild garden with a small summerhouse.

A lasting peace

Buckland Abbey, deep in its secluded valley, blessed with profound tranquillity and natural beauty, has survived for more than seven centuries, witness to great change over that time while preserving much of its original character.

The monastic complex, built by the will and faith of Abbot Robert and his seven monks, included a prosperous estate, producing meat, grain and timber to further the Cistercian foundation.

Times changed. The monks were cast out in the 16th century as Henry VIII broke away from Rome, ordering his chancellor Thomas Cromwell to dissolve the monasteries. Buckland became a private residence. The soaring walls supporting the vaulted nave of the abbey church were split, horizontally, into three to create chambers for family occupation.

It became the home for a short while of flamboyant adventurer Sir Richard Grenville, followed by that great seaman, Sir Francis Drake, who valued his country retreat as much for its proximity to the sea as for its peace and solitude. Generations of Drakes came and went, leaving their own imprint. In more recent history, fire destroyed part of the mansion, but Buckland continued.

Buried beneath stone and bricks, plaster and panelling, lies the beating heart of the house, part of the old abbey church. In its walls are the distant echoes of the prayers and chanting of the faithful Cistercian monks, from the time over seven hundred years ago, when they moved to build their abbey in this west Devon valley.

Above Buckland Abbey nestling in its valley as it has done for more than 700 years